B is for Botulism

An Alphabet Book of Words that are Fun to Say

J.W. Kent

Printed in the United States of America

First Printing, 2015

ISBN-13:978-1508614661

This book is for Allura.

And for any child who will giggle at "funny words,"

As well as all adults who delight in words that are fun to say.

A great deal of gratitude is owed to the members of "The Society" for the encouragement that led to this book.

A: Is for

Anthropomorphism, Anarchy, and Ale

B: Is for

Botulism,

Bailiwick,

and Bale

C: Is for

Cenozoic,

Capricious,

and Conflagrate

D: is for

Diastrophism,

Desiccated,

and Deflate

E: Is for

Entropy,

Escarpment,

and Eschew

F: Is for

Fastidious,

Fermentation,

and Flue

G: Is for

Geomorphology, Gauntlet, and Gael

H: Is for

Harlequin,
Hellgrammite,
and Hale

I: Is for

Inexorable,

Impervious,

and Imbibe

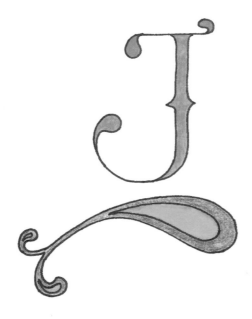

J: Is for

Jurassic,

Jaundiced,

and Jibe

K: Is for

Kinetic,

Kettle,

and Karst

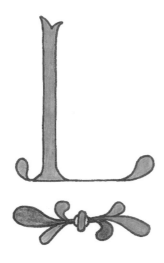

L: Is for

Laccolith,

Larboard,

and Larch

M: Is for

Miocene,

Mead,

and Musket

N: Is for

Neolithic,

Necromancy,

and Nantucket

O: Is for

Ordovician,

Overt,

and Obstreperous

P: Is for

Primordial,

Parapet,

and Preposterous

Q: Is for

Quagmire,

Quandary,

and Quark

R: Is for

Rapscallion,

Ribald,

and Remark

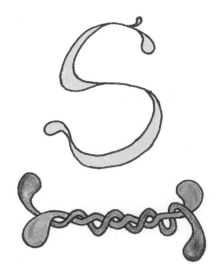

S: is for

Sagacious,

Sedition,

and Strident

T: Is for

Troglodyte, Tertiary, and Trident

U: Is for

Ubiquitous,

Ungulate,

and Umber

V: Is for

Veracity,

Viscous,

and Visor

W: Is for

Wainwright,

Wattle,

and Wretch

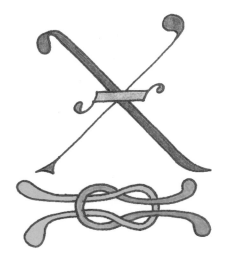

X: Is for

Xenolith,
Xerophyte,
and Xebec

Y: Is for

Yarrow,

Yeoman,

and Yen

Z: Is for

Zymurgy,

Zephyr,

and Zen

Anthropomorphism: The ascribing of human characteristics to inanimate objects, animals, or natural phenomena.

Anarchy: Lack of any political authority.

Ale: Beer made with any of several strains of top fermenting yeast.

Botulism: Acute food poisoning caused by bacteria.

Bailiwick: One's special sphere or province.

Bale: A large bound bundle, or package.

Cenozoic: The current and most recent of the three Phanerozoic geological eras, following the Mesozoic Era, and covering the period from 66 million years ago to the present.

Capricious: Given to sudden and unaccountable changes of mood or behavior.

Conflagrate: Cause to start burning.

Diastrophism: Large-scale deformation of the Earth's crust by natural processes, which leads to the formation of continents and ocean basins, mountain systems, plateaus, rift valleys, and other features by mechanisms such as plate tectonics, volcanic loading, or folding.

Desiccated: Dried, with the moisture removed.

Deflate: Let air or gas out of a tire, balloon, or similar object.

Entropy: Lack of order or predictability; gradual decline into disorder.

Escarpment: A long, steep slope, especially one at the edge of a plateau or separating areas of land at different heights.

Eschew: Deliberately avoid using; abstain from.

Fastidious: Very attentive to and concerned about accuracy and detail.

Fermentation: A metabolic process that converts sugar to acids, gases, and/or alcohol.

Flue: A duct, pipe, or opening in a chimney for conveying exhaust gases from a fireplace, furnace, water heater, boiler, or generator to the outdoors.

Geomorphology: The scientific study of the origin and evolution of topographic and bathymetric features created by physical or chemical processes operating at or near Earth's surface.

Gauntlet: Protective gloves used as a form of armor.

Gael: A Scottish Celt or Highlander.

Harlequin: A character in comedy and pantomime with a shaved head, masked face, variegated tights, and wooden sword.

Hellgrammite: The aquatic larva of the dobsonfly.

Hale: (of a person, especially an elderly one) Strong and healthy.

Inexorable: Impossible to stop or prevent.

Impervious: Incapable of being penetrated.

Imbibe: To drink, take in, or   absorb.

Jurassic: Geologic period and system that extends from 201.3 million years ago to 145 million years ago.

Jaundiced: Affected by a yellowish staining of the eyes and skin.

Jibe: To shift the wind from one side of a sailing vessel to the other across the stern.

Kinetic: Of, pertaining to, or produced by motion.

Kettle: A metal pot used for boiling.

Karst: An area of irregular limestone where erosion has produced caverns, and underground streams.

Laccolith: A mass of igneous rock intruded between layers of sedimentary rock.

Larboard: Nautical term for left; port.

Larch: A coniferous tree with deciduous needles.

Miocene: Geologic time period from 23.03 to 5.33 million years ago.

Mead: An alcoholic beverage made from honey.

Musket: A smoothbore military firearm fired from the shoulder.

Neolithic: "New Stone Age" This Era, or Period, was a period in the development of human technology, beginning about 10,200 BC.

Necromancy: Communication with the dead to foretell the future.

Nantucket: An island 30 miles (50 km) south of Cape Cod, in the American state of Massachusetts.

Ordovician: A Geologic time period of the Paleozoic Era, from 485.4 to 443.4 million years ago.

Overt: Not hidden or concealed.

Obstreperous: Noisy and unruly, especially in defiance.

Primordial: Existing first, or in an original state.

Parapet: An embankment or rampart to protect soldiers.

Preposterous: Beyond all reason, absurd.

Quagmire: Land with a soft, yielding surface.

Quandary: A perplexing situation, or state.

Quark: An elementary particle and a fundamental constituent of matter.

Rapscallion: A rascal.

Ribald: Marked by, or indulging in coarse humor.

Remark: A casual or brief expression of opinion.

Sagacious: Marked by keen perception; wise.

Sedition: Behavior or language that brings about rebellion.

Strident: Harsh, grating, and loud.

Troglodyte: A cave dweller, one who lives in a cave.

Tertiary: Third in place, order, degree, or rank. Formerly, a geologic time period.

Trident: A long, three pointed weapon, or spear.

Ubiquitous: Being, or seeming to be everywhere.

Ungulate: Having hoofs.

Umber: A natural brown earth used as pigment.

Veracity: Devotion to the truth.

Viscous: Having a relatively high resistance to flow; thick.

Visor: The front piece of a helmet, able to be raised and lowered.

Wainwright: One who make wagons.

Wattle: Sticks and twigs woven into a construction material, as for walls and fences.

Wretch: A miserable or contemptible person.

Xenolith: A rock fragment foreign to the igneous mass in which it occurs.

Xerophyte: A plant adapted to growing in an environment providing limited moisture.

Xebec: A three-masted sailing ship with both square and triangular sails used in the Mediterranean.

Yarrow: A type of pungent smelling plant.

Yeoman: An independent farmer below the noble class.

Yen: A longing or yearning.

Zymurgy: The science that deals with fermentation, as in brewing.

Zephyr: A gentle breeze.

Zen: A form of Buddhism that reaches enlightenment through meditation.

About the author:

J.W. Kent is the author of the sword and sorcery fantasy series The Legend of Fergus. He is a Bluegrass musician and avid homebrewer. He also enjoys fishing, black powder firearms, playing his bagpipes and doting on his granddaughter. He makes his home in the Shenandoah Valley with his wife Robin, and can not imagine a life without dogs in it.

Visit the author at:

http://www.deadpixelpublications.com/jw-kent

https://www.goodreads.com/JWKent

https://www.facebook.com/jw.kent.71

Also by J.W. Kent:

Available at Amazon in both print, and Kindle versions

The Legend of Fergus: *(Fantasy)*

The Bridge at Ardendale

The Wind from the Islands

The Bards Will Sing

The Fields of Valdenheim
With Fire and Sword

Ashes of Wrath (Forthcoming)

***

Patina (Sci-Fi short story)

The Ravens Claw (Horror short story)

You've been enjoying a DeadPixel Publications Book.

DeadPixel Publications is a group of people with day jobs, writing for the pure love of the craft and hoping for a little success along the way. By joining forces we help promote each other and create a community of sharing and collaboration with one goal in mind: Helping the public find some kick ass books to read (if we do say so ourselves).

Please visit our website.

www.deadpixelpublications.com

Made in United States
Troutdale, OR
03/11/2024

18392815R00026